THE TRIDENT POEMS

THE TRIDENT POEMS

Korkut Onaran

World Enough
Writers

Copyright © 2018 Korkut Onaran

All rights reserved. No part of this publication may be reproduced distributed or transmitted in any form or by any means whatsoever without written permission from the publisher, except in the case of brief excerpts for critical reviews and articles. All inquiries should be addressed to World Enough Writers.

Poetry
ISBN 978-1-937797-05-8

Cover art: photo by Korkut Onaran

Author photo: courtesy of Jennifer B. Frank

Design: Tonya Namura
using Book Antiqua and Gill Sans

World Enough Writers is dedicated to publishing themed poetry anthologies and special selected collections of the finest poets anywhere.

World Enough Writers
PO Box 445
Tillamook, OR 97141

WorldEnoughWriters@gmail.com

http://WorldEnoughWriters.com

ACKNOWLEDGEMENTS

The author thanks and acknowledges the following publications where some of the poems in this collection have previously appeared:

"A Bird" in *Cold Mountain Review*

"A Contemplative Conversation" in *Front Range Review*

"Of Being in the Present" in *Common Ground Review*

"Of Water" in *Common Ground Review*

"Overhearing Those Around Me" in *Lalitamba*

"Sunshine After the Storm" in *Evening Street Review*

TABLE OF CONTENTS

AUTHOR'S PREFACE	xiii

YEAR OF THE DRAGON: I TOOK A WALK TO MYSELF

I TOOK A WALK TO MYSELF	5
A NOCTURNAL ODE	7
OF THE BIRD AND THE FISH	8
THE PEAR	9
OF BEING IN THE PRESENT	10
A NOTE ON LOVE	11
OF SUBURBIA	12
OF OCTOBER	13
SCRIBBLES	14
LOVE SONG THAT LOOKS LIKE A CARVED PUMPKIN	16
ODE TO DON EDUARDO	17
OVERHEARING	18
MEANWHILE	19
MY DEATH	20

YEAR OF THE SNAKE: FACEGAZING

FACEGAZING	23
ON THE MEANING OF FUTURE	24
ODE TO AN APRIL MORNING	25
THIS PLACE	26
A MID-MAY POEM	27
A MEMORY OF MINE	28
SUMMER RAIN	29
WHAT GOES INTO THE POEM	31
A BIRD	32
"SSH!"	33
ONCE IN A THOUSAND YEARS	34
EN PASSANT	35
AMNESIA	36

YEAR OF THE HORSE: A CONTEMPLATIVE CONVERSATION

OF A WINTER DAY	39
A CONTEMPLATIVE CONVERSATION	40
A NON-POEM	41
IN THE SKY	42
ME AND A MINUTE	43
THE SMALL GREEN TEA CUP	44
WRITING OF YOU AGAIN	45
HIS LAST FUGUE	46

YEAR OF THE SHEEP: PEOPLE THOUGHT I WAS A POET

IN OUR NEW TALL BED	49
PEOPLE THOUGHT I WAS A POET	50
A LATE APRIL AFTERNOON WEATHERTALK	51
LIGHT RAIN	52
THIS SUNDAY AFTERNOON	53
A DECEMBER SUNRISE	54

YEAR OF THE MONKEY: BEING BUSY

BEING BUSY	57
BRUEGEL'S FACES	58
URLICHT	59
SICK AT PAPALLACTA HOT SPRINGS, ECUADOR	60
HAFIZ	61
OVERHEARING THOSE AROUND ME	62
AN APRIL POEM	64
WHO WE ARE	65
TODAY'S COLORS	66
AN ODE TO M. K. ATATÜRK	68
OF WATER	69
THE SPARROW	70
FICTION	71
AN AUTHOBIOGRAPHICAL NOTE	72

YEAR OF THE ROOSTER: SO MANY POSSIBILITIES!

A CROWDED AFTERNOON IN THE TRIDENT	75
AN EARLY MARCH MORNING	77
SUNSHINE AFTER THE STORM	78
SO MANY POSSIBILITIES!	79
THE MAN AND THE MIRROR	80
SKYGAZING	81
JASMINE PEARLS	82
ABOUT THE AUTHOR	85

AUTHOR'S PREFACE

Wealth of Nations by Adam Smith, *Principia* by Isaac Newton, *Lettres Philosophique* by François-Marie Voltaire, *Encyclopédie* by Denis Diderot, *The Social Contract* by Jean-Jacques Rousseau — all conceived and written in coffeehouses! Thinkers then met, discussed, and even lectured in coffeehouses. Some had their mail delivered to coffeehouses.

Well, those days are over. Nevertheless, when you visit the Trident there is something in the air that reminds you of the Enlightenment Era of coffeehouses' glory. In the Trident there are words. Many of them! Some in the form of chatter, some in minds not yet spoken, some are landing on the notebooks, and others are already landed on the pages of the printed books that are quietly looking at you from their shelves.

This modest book is dedicated to all these words.

Raise your words, not voice. It is rain that grows flowers, not thunder.
— Rumi

The words you speak become the house you live in.
— Hafiz

THE TRIDENT POEMS

YEAR OF THE DRAGON:
I TOOK A WALK TO MYSELF

I TOOK A WALK TO MYSELF

I took a walk to myself
as a moon would on a lake.
The streets of the forest
turned and turned.
The buildings looked like trees.
My shadow did not know my name.
I did not know where I was. Yet,
I was content.

Then I arrived at a place so dark
that my eyes bled a heavy silence;
the kind you find in caves
where only the most fragile petals
of your psyche can hear the blue
hidden in the dark.

I took a walk to myself
as moss would on a trunk.
The ground was covered by touches.
There were fingers instead of words.
Touches shaped my thoughts.
It took some time
to become familiar. But then
it felt okay.

I arrived at a hibiscus garden.
Each offered me their red,
yellow, orange. It felt as if
I was the light; as if all I was seeing
was coming out of my own eyes. I was fragile,
open, porous, yet somehow strong.

I took a walk to myself
as a metaphor would in a poem.
There was an ocean in my sky

to which rivers of dreams ran.
Some of the rivers were frozen.
A fish, slow, hardly alive,
was sitting on the bottom of a river.

I took a walk to myself
and walked and walked.
I filled volumes of notebooks
and I was only
at the beginning.

February 21, 2012
The Trident

A NOCTURNAL ODE

The mountains' shadow
grows ambitious
and takes in the whole city.
The mountains' shadow
grows more ambitious
and takes in the eastern plains.
The mountains' shadow
announces the night
as a work of shadows.

Stars appear on the plain
and the sky mirrors them.
Glitter settles on the eyelids
of the sleeping forest.
A kid flies a kite, in his dream,
that looks like the moon.
The moonlight sits on a lake
and an owl hears it.

Then, after a complete silence
that endures itself no one knows how long,
the expected happens unexpectedly:
from the pores of the skin
of all things
the morning oozes into the world.

March 3, 2012
The Trident

OF THE BIRD AND THE FISH

A bird is circling. The poem
follows the bird into the water
so fast that it becomes the fish.

The fish swims through the poet's body
when he is asleep, dreaming
of ocean's depths with titanic distances.

The poem grows strong and takes over
the poet's life. First his name abandons him.
Then, he becomes the fish.

March 27, 2012
The Trident

THE PEAR

A small bruise from a touch!
Behind the darker skin
where it is sweeter and softer
and where the alcohol carries
the intoxicating luscious essence
of being alive,
there the poem
finds metaphors for constant dying
and procreation.
Then, the poem takes a bite
and juice runs from
the corners
of her mouth.

May 6, 2012
The Trident

OF BEING IN THE PRESENT

I

I keep running
to catch up with the present.
But it has a motorcycle; it moves
faster than my running.
At the back seat of the bike
is my absence
waving at me.
I am exhausted.
I stop
and gaze into the sky for a while
unaware that I've actually just
entered the present.

II

I make poems.
Then tomorrow comes
and none of my poems are in it.
So I start making poems again.
Then the next day comes
and my poems are not in it.
So I start again.
On and on
I live for years
like this.

June 16, 2012
The Trident

A NOTE ON LOVE
to Martina and Fernando

Love is
the coziness
of sitting close to a fire
in a cottage at a small mountain village
during a wild storm.
Love is
also the storm itself
and the face of the cliff
standing against the storm.

June 30, 2012
The Trident

OF SUBURBIA

A highway passes through
a city without arriving.

A giant building asks for its name
to each car driving by.

A group of dreams moves
into an office park.

A roadside landscaped boulder asks for the time.
There is nobody around to reply that it is always
    noon there.

A word on the sign
does not remember its meaning.

A mild nevertheless aggresive
form of schizophrenia enters the city,

while a mother of three,
alone, late morning,

sits at the breakfast table
and cries quietly.

July 15, 2012
The Trident

OF OCTOBER

October
composes
orange
poems.

Even though nowadays
it is the tenth month,
an eight-legged metaphor
still lives in October.

October is the month when
ocean, octopus, and the goddess of love
meet in the center of the letter 'o'
and have an orgy.

Too, in October death wears
many colors and so do the sunsets
while life takes
relaxing walks in cemeteries.

Life paints its face
and celebrates
death
on October's last day.

October 14, 2012
The Trident

SCRIBBLES

I

I take off my clothes.
Then I take off my memories.
Take off my worries
and my to do lists.
I lie down
there
selfless.
Yet my pen
continues to scribble.

II

I throw myself
into the creek
and sink
as a pebble.
I live there for a while
with water running
over my colors;
nothing else, but
just water
running
and running.

III

I listen to
the red zebra jasper necklace
I wear over my chest bone.
I study
the way it relates to time.

It tells me that if I moved
very fast
the stone would feel like air.
And if I moved really
slowly
the air would feel
like stone.

IV

I get up,
put on my clothes,
put on my memories, worries,
to do lists,
shave,
refresh,
leave, arrive,
get a pot of tea,
sit down,
and read my scribbles.

V

I reach
my absence.
I build
a strong friendship
with my absence.

October 20, 2012
The Trident

LOVE SONG THAT LOOKS LIKE A CARVED PUMPKIN

Wear a mask for me
that, when I look at you, tastes like
mango and passion fruit.

Then come to bed
and speak to me of curves
that shape my will.

Meet me at that ridge
between living and dying
and let's go back and forth.

But most of all kiss me
on my tomorrow,
and on my day after tomorrow.

Let us die then,
in this late hour of the colorful night,
an ant-sized orange death.

November 2, 2012
The Trident

ODE TO DON EDUARDO

A good añejo
should look like rich pee
of the sunset color
over a spicy ocean.
Its aroma should be
like a complex memory.
It should taste spacious
and as busy as the jungle.
It should, in the mouth,
create succulence
like a tropical cloud
that keeps hanging in the air.
It should accommodate the words
smoke, oak, smooth, and skin
in the same sentence with
the scent of love.
It should speak of dew living
an aged life on the skin
of a tropical leaf.
Once it gets
comfortable in your thought
and reaches the cheeks of your initials
it should convince you
of the reasons
for civilization.

November 4, 2012
The Trident

OVERHEARING

A heated conversation
at the next table.
He did this. He did that.
He was such a …. And
Oh my God! I was like ….

Then they left.
A restless silence
lingered.

Among the unbussed cups
and napkins on their table
there were words left behind.
Many "likes," exclamations,
unfinished sentences….
All waiting to be swept
away, to be
forgotten.

November 17, 2012
The Trident

MEANWHILE

Sometimes simultaneities
try to get into my poem.
A kid on the next block
falls down, tripping on the sidewalk.
Meanwhile in the sky
clouds, colorful clouds!
I let them in.

A teenager walks into the coffeehouse
with a little white fluffy dog on her lap.
Dust on the ledge.
And a tongue touches
the melting ice cream—no, not mine,
it's at a warm beach
miles and months away.

And as if all this is not enough
my eighty-year-old future self
remembers this very moment.
Meanwhile one of my poems,
yet to be composed, rises,
as if to leave gravity and reach
where my absence occupies
all places
simultaneously.

November 24, 2012
The Trident

MY DEATH

I want to die a simple death.
Not a giant or flamboyant one.
Not an absurd and wasteful one either.
I want to die a simple
and a familiar death.
A quiet one.
It may be light blue
or white
but not orange
or purple.
It is okay if it is
nameless.
It is okay if it happens
while I cloud gaze.
I want to die when
my mind is busy
composing
a death poem.

December 16, 2012
The Trident.

YEAR OF THE SNAKE:
FACEGAZING

FACEGAZING

A memory of an evening breeze
joins me at my table
and we gaze together
at the familiar faces around us.

Some faces say "hi" to us. We say
"hi" to them. They are the familiar faces
but their dreams are naked today. I realize
how unique each body shape is.

I also notice that there are all sorts of
creatures in these dreams; eels,
sparrows, giant sea turtles,
intentions about to be transformed

into colorful butterflies....
Some lips let go cherry sized words
into the room, freely.
I see the scent of tangerine on the edge

of a very voluptuous mouth.
I say to myself:
If I didn't keep writing these down
none

would make sense to me.

January 25, 2013
The Trident

ON THE MEANING OF FUTURE

Future is full of reconciliations,
miracles, and surprises.
This is why it doesn't come
often. It is shy. It takes its time.

I wonder if I'll live long enough
to see it. I also wonder what
makes it this shy. Is it something
that I am doing? Or not doing?

What if the future is a metaphor
for Odysseus's return? But what if he is
already dead? Or having eternal fun with a
perfect nymph of his desire's imagination?

I see an apple, hanging in the air motionless
in front of my future face.
I take a bite
and stop wondering.

March 24, 2013
The Trident

ODE TO AN APRIL MORNING

Clouds play
shadow games
on the plains.

Light moves
like a kiss
and bounces on many lips.

In the air
a crisp fresh aura of
willingness.

I close my eyes
and feel the air
on my eyelids.

April 7, 2013
Trident

THIS PLACE

The entrance of this coffee house!
I have been here so many times.
But only now I see that it looks
like a face that remembers who I am.

I see my gaze reflected as well
on this façade composition as if to confirm
an affinity; I think this brick wall remembers names
from my past that even I don't remember.

This is how this place moves into my language
and gets comfortable reclining on the idea
of who I am. I too sometimes recline on the idea
of who I am. Maybe this is why I keep coming here.

April 20, 2013
The Trident

A MID-MAY POEM

Some changes happen slowly
yet so fast.
They don't make any sound.
Still, you need to listen to them carefully.

It's mid-May already and trees across the street
are yet to bloom. Nevertheless, there is
in the air
chirpings, warmth, and sex.

It's mid-life and there are
fruits yet to ripen.
There are also almond blossoms
somewhere in my thought.

I must be part of what
I imagine.

May 14, 2013
The Trident

A MEMORY OF MINE

I take a memory of mine
for a walk
through some metaphors—
my memories like metaphors.

We run into a minute that is
larger than its hour. There,
I see a mirror, in which
my future face gazes back at me.

In my gaze I see yours too.
And your gaze tells me that
your absence will meet mine
and they will fall in love too.

I draw from my pocket
some moonlight and let
my memory wear it.
Then I enter my memory

and start swimming
in a dark, wine-drunk sea
next to you—I am exactly
the way you remember me.

July 3, 2013
The Trident

SUMMER RAIN

A raindrop!

Another one!

I keep reading.

Tiny splashes
land on my page—
they bounce from the larger drops
landing on the table.
I keep reading.

After a while I realize
that my sandals
are getting wet.
People on the sidewalk
start running.
I keep reading

without really
comprehending what I'm reading.
I close the book
and gaze upon the rain.

I decide
to transform myself
into a raindrop

and travel
back in time.

Eventually I reach
my cloud.

July 13, 2013
The Trident

WHAT GOES INTO THE POEM

I take into the poem
some deep blue patches of sky,
a few tall western clouds,
and their giant evening shadows.
I take in
this unexpectedly strong gust and the way
it knocks over some signs, blows away napkins,
and explores the agility of short summer dresses.

I take in barefoot gazes and naked steps
along with their thoughts
and waterfall-like intentions.
I take in a few kisses, select touches,
lips and a few nipple-shaped syllables.
I take in a sparrow, a lady bug,
and a raindrop.

I invite from far away the song
of a dolphin, the ink of an octopus,
and a few sea breezes good for easy sailing.

Then I take a break
and leave the poem alone for awhile.

I pretend I am not watching.
I pretend I am cloud gazing instead.

Meanwhile I keep taking notes.

July 20, 2013
The Trident

A BIRD

I draw from my pocket
a metaphor; unarticulated,
young, inexperienced,
yet eager to move ahead.

It hops around the table
like a small bird.
Just when I start taking notes
it flies away.

I will never know
of its desires, thoughts,
habits,
or even its name.

August 16, 2013
The Trident

"SSH!"
after Rolf Jaconsen

A feminine moon
impregnates the poem.

Through some
complicated metaphors
the poem gives birth
to an orange silence.

"Ssh!" says the poem,
"this is my orange silence."

September 7, 2013
The Trident

ONCE IN A THOUSAND YEARS

The poem is flooded with waters coming up
from the soil—how did I forget it on the ground?

Nothing drains! Words are soaked!
Whispers, continuous whispers in the walls!

Just when exclamations start to dry
more water comes in.

Stop reading this; your clothes
will start to stink!

There is a drought in this flood.
We need to move to a higher ground!

September 15, 2013
The Trident

EN PASSANT

An orange explanation
for why pleasure is a right
meets a bishop on a chess board.
The chess board has never seen a color.

A white and a black pawn keep staring at each other.
The bishop is taken out on the next move.
The black king sees an orange exclamation mark
in his dream.

The single bishop left on the board
imagines a water fall
strong enough to flood the minds of teenagers.
He too is taken out on the next move.

The white queen
joins an innocent fairy tale.
The black queen imagines a book
whose words fly away in the wind.

The white pawn
takes out the black pawn
not even touching him —
o, so conveniently!

Meanwhile, outside,
a colorful sunset
invites the planet
to the end game.

September 15, 2013
The Trident

AMNESIA

Something happens
and we all forget
how to talk to each other;
how to relate,
share, pay attention.

A collective fear floods the streets
and people, each as an individual,
walk up and down the town,
avoiding each other's eyes,
hoping that something will happen.

Somebody falls down.
People gather around thinking
that they need to do something.
But what?
Nobody remembers.

The tension is
unbearable!

November 23, 2013
The Trident

YEAR OF THE HORSE:
A CONTEMPLATIVE CONVERSATION

OF A WINTER DAY

Snowflakes don't recognize
their bodies as distinct anymore;
they fill the sky
all at once,
as if all minutes are one
and the same.

The silence
doesn't remember anything either.
It's just a white day,
with a white sky,
where white words land
on the white pages of winter.

In this scene
the question of where we are
is written in the margins
in fine print.
As a matter of fact, there are already
too many words.

January 4, 2014
The Trident

A CONTEMPLATIVE CONVERSATION

Here sits next to me
a friendly talkative silence.
It glows like a night sky
hungry for bright colors.

It tells me that sometimes
there is this space
in between two words,
that craves a blank page.

There are, I reply,
no more empty pages left anywhere.
Besides, I add, nowadays we live
with so much noise pollution.

Nevertheless, the silence tells me,
that it is up to me to clear
space in my poems
to accommodate silences of many colors.

It advises me
to pay attention to
the sound that my pen
makes on the paper.

I listen.
I transform myself and become for a while
the sound
my pen makes on the paper.

June 21, 2014
The Trident

A NON-POEM

He dreams
that he is a flute solo.
He feels on his forehead
the gentle touch of the supporting cellos.
The staccato finger of an oboe
pokes him once in a while.
Finally, the off-key entrance
of a French horn wakes him up.

It takes a few seconds for him
to realize where he is.
He ignores the school of fish
passing by the bedroom.

Then he faces me and asks:
why are you using the third person singular?

Freaked out
is the narrator of the poem.

The poem is taken over
by the passive non-narrator.

No need to go further.

August 2, 2014
The Trident

IN THE SKY

a face!
On it, many metaphors!

A cloud!
On it, many gazes!

Deep thoughts
are expanding
into the late afternoon sky.
There are fireflies in these thoughts.

Is your nose a lavender cloud?
Are your lips winds?
Is there, in your gaze, a sea
of silences in which
one of my future selves swim?

Even the most passionate colors in the sky
are silent,

except
for the evening thunders.

A face
is about to pour
onto my notebook.

August 3, 2014
The Trident

ME AND A MINUTE

A minute
among others
is just being itself
disinterested
in all that sits beyond.

It is round,
brittle,
and self-reserved.
Yet it invites me in
for a cup of tea.

After some small talk,
just when we go
deeper
it rolls down
and passes away.

August 30, 2014
The Trident

THE SMALL GREEN TEA CUP

I am not the only one
with memories;
this small porcelain green tea cup as well
remembers;
the fingertips, lips,
the scent of various teas,
conversations too!

But beyond these, this tea cup
holds memories of the far east, long ago,
even though it has never been
beyond Boulder,
let alone overseas,

it remembers the tea masters
of Medieval China,
their ceremonies,
their haiku;
their metaphors that fit
this cup's small body
perfectly.

It tells me that I may, if I want,
borrow some of its memories.
I smile,
and take another sip.

September 12, 2014
The Trident

WRITING OF YOU AGAIN

Your absence
is sitting at my table with a gaze
that is as strong as the gaze
of a waterfall—I jump in for a cold plunge! —

the orange intensions of your gaze
take me deep into an innerness
where I befriend and become intimate with
our tomorrow

and here you are
calling me on the phone.

September 21, 2014
The Trident

HIS LAST FUGUE

Bach was obsessed with
weaving long sentences into each other;
sentences that went on and on,
several of them,
borrowing each other's clauses,
repeating, in a cyclical
and evolving order, like sex,
moving into a network of reflections;
into an abundance of intelligence,
and all this kept growing, as if
it could never end!

But then, he did end his sentences,
arbitrarily, kind of abruptly,
almost artificially — I guess because
he had a life to go back and live.

But not the last fugue!
He did not finish that one.
He did not want to finish it.
How could he?
He reached a place, outside of time,
where there was no end.

November 16, 2014
The Trident

YEAR OF THE SHEEP:
PEOPLE THOUGHT I WAS A POET

IN OUR NEW TALL BED

Your sleep
bathes
in the river of your hair.

Our ceiling is dusk blue
and it pulls us in
to its constellations.

My thought
walks
the warmth of your curves.

I put my lips
on your sky
and listen

to your ocean
enter
my waterfall.

March 22, 1015
The Trident

PEOPLE THOUGHT I WAS A POET

Last night
I found myself
in a dog's dream.
I was insecure,
and desperate.

Then I ate the sunset.
My words
became so colorful;
the clouds were
listening to me.

Then, behind the clouds,
the moon rose.
It was so impressive
that people thought
I was a poet.

April 20, 2015
The Trident

A LATE APRIL AFTERNOON WEATHERTALK

Cold breeze and warm sunshine
wrestle with each other for the next moment
and the sidewalks keep
putting on and taking off their sweaters.

In the sky storm clouds and patches of blue speak
a confused sentence.
My pen, insisting to sit outside,
keeps maneuvering around occasional raindrops.

The hair on legs stands up
in spite of the sweat at the roots.
Rain sleeps in the mid-air
and its silence reaches the faces

looking up and asking what's next.
The poem doesn't know the answer.

April 25, 2015
The Trident

LIGHT RAIN

The sunlit rain
collects sparkles

and corrals them
into the words

and the poem
dresses emotions

with transparent
overalls

made
of light.

June 28, 2015
The Trident

THIS SUNDAY AFTERNOON

A giant white cloud
moves over the city
casting a white shadow
over all of the metaphors
about to be born.

A fresh afternoon breeze
in A minor
walks the sidewalks
and touches the light green emotions
hidden in the faces.

An October sunset,
lips apart,
eyes cloudy,
heart open,
gazes upon the city.

October 11, 2015
The Trident

A DECEMBER SUNRISE

In the dark each minute anticipates
one more step into a brighter sky.
Colors with red thoughts gather
in the eastern horizon. Soon,
they cover the whole sky.

The first sunlight of the day,
like a newborn's hand,
touches the poem's face.
A compass points to a cloud
and all the metaphors orient.

Some words insist on taking the poem
up into the sky. These words are
larger than their bodies and they make
oceanic waves in a few syllables.
They overwhelm the other words.

The poem decides to leave them outside
and enters the coffeehouse.
Soon, the warm air and the coffee smell
settle
on the notebook.

December 4, 2015
The Trident

YEAR OF THE MONKEY:
BEING BUSY

BEING BUSY

Lately time is hungry.
I keep feeding it and it wants more.
Days go away as if they were spring flowers.
I don't know how much time
remains
but I have a long to do list
each day
and the list
doesn't look like voluptuous clouds;
it doesn't look like young flowers either,
except for Rilke's rose:
to be no one's sleep
behind so many eyelids.

A hummingbird
enters the clock
and confuses
the hell out of time.

February 7, 2016
The Trident

BRUEGEL'S FACES

Pain moves in and settles.
Some of these faces
don't even remember anymore
why it hurts,
or how it all started.

Pain is a part
of the face's ecosystem now
like oxygen,
without which
the heart cannot beat.

And they keep
talking to each other,
moving the cattle,
working the fields,
growing the kids.

From far away
all looks vibrant,
even
cheerful.

February 7, 2016
The Trident

URLICHT
(An ode to Mahler)

On the altar of my solitude
grow intricate metaphors; I
water them each day
with my attention.

A large crane lands on the word
I am about to speak.
A shrimp, in disguise as a rooster,
starts a hidden French horn solo.
Then the ocean enters the concert hall.
The choir grows taller and taller.
Meanwhile, a school of colorful fish
explores the depths of ocean's silence.
A white whale stares at the trombones.
Waves crash, storms flash
and in the middle of all this
a pearl
leaves her oyster
and reaches the sky
to join the stars.

And I,
alone,
away from it all,
live small
with my song,
with my heart,
with my metaphors.

February 21, 2016
The Trident

SICK AT PAPALLACTA HOT SPRINGS, ECUADOR

These creatures are so small
it is hard to believe they exist.
Yet they did enter my body and grew crowded there
and here I am, in bed, with high fewer, thinking
of the weird bumps that showed up on my legs.
It's not like I touch or see these creatures. It feels as if
the story of them being in my body
is more mythological than real.
Yet the hot springs fairies who, just an hour ago,
touched my forehead and kissed my sacrum,
were very real and sensual. Then, I plunged
into the coldest water — it brought my body back to me
and I've been feeling stronger since. I already
see myself getting up tomorrow fresh and new.
And sometime next month I am writing down
these lines somewhere home, probably
at the Trident; reconstructing
this very moment, of me lying here, in bed,
in this high-country valley, where
Fernando and Martina, my friends, brought us.
He will challenge me to write about this.
And I will remember to mention certain details
of which, right now, I am not completely aware,
but nevertheless, taking in to store
in some back room of my memory palace.
And here he is,
just walked in,
to check how I am doing.

February 28, 2016
The Trident

HAFIZ

Body
turns around itself
and around the sun
but does not know of this.
Whereas the poem
is aware of all whirling.
Hafız told me this once.
He was a bit drunk,
he was talking to the clouds,
he thought
I was one of them.

March 5, 2016
The Trident

OVERHEARING THOSE AROUND ME

Flip flops and the feet:
    So, honestly, it's like paying attention
    to it! It's like this, this,
    and this! I mean, it's not a real job!

The flowering street tree:
    You know, I am realizing more and more
    that I need to celebrate myself
    as an artist.

The tree grate:
    It's not like I don't have
    a business model; I can channel myself;
    I can manage my rhythm.

The large loud black SUV driving by slowly:
    I am falling into a silence so deep
    I don't remember anymore
    what my ears are for.

The tiny green tea leaf floating in my cup:
    The day is tender.
    There are speckles of gratitude
    in the air.

The clashing orange and peach pattern on the woman's tights:
    I really don't want to
    not be all over
    this opportunity.

Hot pants:
    Could you take a picture of us,
    together?
    Be sure that the building shows at the back as well.

The clock on the building wall, across the street:
    I come here to watch people.
    You know,
    it's crazy!

April 9, 2016
The Trident

AN APRIL POEM

A tree
that has been busy all its life
being a tree

enters this very moment
as a colorful cloud.
On its branches

are scents of flowers and sounds of birds.
In the sky,
the urgency and the drama of a waterfall!

Spring
touches
the poem.

April 23, 2016
The Trident

WHO WE ARE

What is home?
asks the sparrow who has just
landed on my table.

I am trying to be exactly who I am
says the young woman to her friend;
both are sitting at the next table.

How can I explain to the sparrow that
I live in a house that I call home?
And then there is this coffee house,

this city,
and then there is that city
and that country….

You are always exactly who you are
replies the shop window.

As she gazes into the window
an exclamation mark lands
on her young face.

One of the books in the window is titled
History of Vegetables.

April 24, 2016
The Trident

TODAY'S COLORS

This morning
from who knows what dream
I woke up with a C major anger
behind my earlobe. I washed it away
but after a subtle modification
it came back in G major.
I just ignored it.

Driving to Denver
I was in a gray hour; outside the car was
wet and slushy. Yet, my mind
was already in the next hour.
The car drove by itself
into the next hour.

In the class
a psychedelic exclamation mark
sailed from heart to heart.
Then, we were there;
in the Mediterranean waters.
There were tiny colorful sea shells
in the words we spoke.
I enjoyed the class.

And now I am in Trident,
drinking green tea and thinking
A minor thoughts.
Some blue intentions loiter in the air;
maybe they are waiting to be fulfilled

or maybe they just like to hang out.
A yellow minute in the corner
is waiting for its turn.

April 30, 2016
The Trident

AN ODE TO M. K. ATATÜRK

Even he himself
left himself alone!
That's how lonely he was.

How else could he be
such a practical idealist?

How else could he know the answers
before anybody realized
there were questions?

He decided to be a gift for us
and so he left himself alone.

And now he is everywhere;
we petrified his words on his sculptures
that we put everywhere. Yet,

he is as alone
as he ever has been.

July 3, 2016
The Trident

OF WATER

I was water once
I flowed, I gathered, I precipitated,
shaped shores, made rainbows,
formed mountains, melted into oceans

I was water once
I took life, I gave life
I was everywhere
in the air, on the plains,

visited bodies of all sorts of creatures,
visited dreams, paintings, epics,
I was water
I was creation

And now, as I sit here
and drink my tea,
raindrops
are landing on my notebook.

July 3, 2016
The Trident

THE SPARROW

In my dream a sparrow dreams
he is a snake; he can't fly.
It feels uncomfortable
yet in a weird way it is
liberating too.

I decide to wake him up, I try to
tell him that snake
is a dream, he really is
a sparrow.

But I am asleep
myself. Then again, maybe
it is my pen; my pen
tells me than I am asleep.

Just when I am convinced
that I am awake
the sparrow lands on my table
and wakes me up.

August 21, 2016
The Trident

FICTION

I don't know why
but one of the characters
killed in a Dostoyevsky novel
shows up in my poem.
She is agitated. She tells me
that she doesn't want
the reader to know about her.
Well too late;
they already know, I tell her.
(I am fully aware
that this will not work; she
doesn't belong here.)
I take her
to a Tennessee Williams play.
She soon joins the play
as the mean aunt. She exposes
the innocent secret lovers and curses
their forbidden love.
The audience doesn't like her.
She knows that.
She starts insulting them
as they leave the theater
one by one.
Tennessee is confused.
He stops writing
and she disappears.
But then
the play doesn't end.

October 15, 2016
The Trident.

AN AUTHOBIOGRAPHICAL NOTE

I love the cast-away
islands I keep inside.

Each morning I go to one of them
for a while.

The remoteness teaches me
to be a foreigner again;

to look at faces
and meet all that is around

as if
for the first time.

October 30, 2016
The Trident

YEAR OF THE ROOSTER:
SO MANY POSSIBILITIES!

A CROWDED AFTERNOON IN THE TRIDENT

A few backgammon games are in progress
to remind me of the tea houses
by the shore where I still call home.
I can hear in the sound of the dice
the deep blue of the Mediterranean waters.

There are the usual laptops too:
the islands of solitudes
isolated in a world crowded
by billions of zeros and ones
flying in the air and bringing
so many virtual spaces
into this coffee house.

As always there are faces too!
Some faces are like deserts;
you walk for miles
and nothing changes.
Some faces are like those
ancient Amazon fighters;
their reserved beauty was created
three thousand years ago.
Some faces are dominated
by their eyebrows;
they say something
even when they don't speak.
Some faces are dominated
by their mouths.

There is an open mouth
at that table over there.
Looks like it has spoken
all the words it held in it

and now there is nothing left to say.
Next to it is a mouth that
never runs out of words.

And many words in the air
traveling this way and that!
Words in all sorts of colors, sizes, and shapes!
In spite of all the noise in the coffee house
there is also a deep silence.

Only a few of us
are aware of it
and actually can hear it.

Mine usually hides
in the crevices of my jasmine pearls tea.
I take a sip and listen.

February 25, 2017
The Trident

AN EARLY MARCH MORNING

It is warm, sunny, and fresh
as if no atrocities
are being committed in this world.
Trees are eager to bloom
and the soil is hungry for procreation.

A sinking ship appears in the sky
and slowly approaches like a dream.
As it lands on the street everybody
slows down
and levitates
as if we all are
under the water.
A squirrel jumps
and never lands.
The sun pales a bit.
Shadows become softer.

We act as if all this
is very natural.
We keep ignoring the ship.

March 9, 2017
The Trident

SUNSHINE AFTER THE STORM

Just yesterday snowflakes were pelting
against my face. And now,
in this cheery end-of-April afternoon,
tight leggings on young legs claim the sidewalks.

There is sex in the way sun's warmth
touches faces. And the flower petals
lying on the pavement tell me that
a journalist with a blooming mind

—someone I could have met next month—
is being arrested right this moment back home
for announcing to the rulers that there is sex
in the way sun's warmth touches faces.

April 30, 2017
The Trident

SO MANY POSSIBILITIES!

The sky is wearing no make-up this morning.
Sun is naked, and the mountains
look as crisp as a pristine pebble beach.

To the east, small fluffy minutes run
along a river of distances
and reach the horizon.

In front of me is a blank page,
white, wide, abundant.
In it I can go anywhere.

Where should I go? To a back street in İstanbul?
To Ephesus in the second century?
Into a sesame seed? Or should I

walk the refreshing curves
of an orange metaphor? Maybe I should
float my thought in my cup of green tea

or visit an owl's stargazing
or enter the dream of a ladybug
sleeping in moon's shadow.

How about reclining for a nap
in the middle of the letter 'o'
of the 'poem'?

So many possibilities!
And I haven't even started yet.

November 11, 2017
The Trident

THE MAN AND THE MIRROR

He stares at himself
as if seeing the face in the mirror
for the first time; as if trying
to find out who the face belongs to.

He stares so intensely
that finally the image in the mirror
turns around
and walks away.

Now the mirror
holds a void.
He is terrified
but he keeps staring.

A trace of subtle intrigue
appears on his face — it seems like
he finds some answers
in the void.

November 29, 2017
The Trident

SKYGAZING

In this
grammatically questionable
warm and sunny December afternoon
I dare to sit at an outside table on the sidewalk
as an exclamation mark.

Like a sunflower, I turn my face to the sun
and sun's fingertips touch my face
like a kiss
in a foreign language
that I've never heard before.

Fresh snow on the mountaintops! Their
decisive presence assures ours too. The blue,
all over the sky,
is so intense and so abundant!
It reaches my pen and takes it over.

In blue's memory
moments swim
in aquamarine and turquoise waters
where ancient fairies gaze upon us
with their green jade eyes

and they invite us
to play with them,
to string with them, in the depths of the sky,
a necklace
of little shiny eternities.

December 10, 2017
The Trident

JASMINE PEARLS

This morning the dark sky kept thinking
of how cold the eternity would be.
Thoughts
were frozen to my windshield too.

Then the day rose out of the eastern horizon,
warm and sunny, and the winds
—crazy winds—pulled and pushed the hours
hoping to skip one or two.

And now the images are word-gazing
through the jasmine pearls
in the depths of this Trident evening.
My daydreaming opens a tiny hole

on the surface of the minute
and other minutes enter the moment
as I go back and forth between decades.
The lights at the back patio

are on, yellow and soft. Was it fifteen years ago,
in an August evening,
Sherefe played on the patio
while my pen kept scribbling

through the bits and pieces of old
songs accumulating on the table?
Or was it in an August evening
yet to come?

And you, dear reader of a distant
tomorrow on an August evening,
before they enter your thought
keep these lines on your lips for a while.

Then smell the air you keep
in between the letters of your name.
There, taste the jasmine pearls.
Mmm!

Keep in touch.

December 27, 2017
The Trident

ABOUT THE AUTHOR

Korkut Onaran received the First Prize in Cervena Barva Press 2007 Chapbook Contest for *The Book of Colors*, and Second Prize in 2006 *Baltimore Review* Poetry Competition for his poem "House." His poetry has been published in journals such as *Penumbra, Rhino, Peralta, Colere, Writer's Journal, White Pelican Review, Crucible, City Works Literary Journal, Water~Stone, Review, Atlanta Review, The Cape Rock, Common Ground Review,* and *Baltimore Review*.

Korkut owns an urban planning and architecture firm with his business partner Ronnie Pelusio in Boulder, Colorado. He teaches as an assistant professor adjunct in the University of Colorado at Denver. His book *Crafting Form-Based Codes: Design, Policy, and Regulation* will be published by Routledge in summer, 2018.

Korkut, originally from Turkey, moved to Madison, Wisconsin, in 1991. After he completed his doctorate studies in 1996, he moved to Colorado. He lives with his wife Jennifer B. Frank in Longmont, Colorado.

www.ingramcontent.com/pod-product-compliance
Lightning Source LLC
Chambersburg PA
CBHW021445080526
44588CB00009B/695